The
World's Best
Skiing Jokes

In this series:

The World's Best Dirty Jokes
More of the World's Best Dirty Jokes
Still More of the World's Best Dirty Jokes
The World's Best Irish Jokes
More of the World's Best Irish Jokes
Still More of the World's Best Irish Jokes
The World's Best Jewish Jokes
More of the World's Best Jewish Jokes
The World's Best Doctor Jokes
More of the World's Best Doctor Jokes
The World's Best Dirty Stories
The World's Best Dirty Limericks
The World's Best Dirty Songs
The World's Best Aussie Jokes
The World's Best Catholic Jokes
The World's Best Mother-in-Law Jokes
The World's Best Russian Jokes
The World's Best Fishing Jokes
The World's Best Salesman Jokes
The World's Best Scottish Jokes
The World's Best Cricket Jokes
The World's Best Golf Jokes
More of the World's Best Golf Jokes
The World's Best Lawyer Jokes
The World's Best Business Jokes
The World's Best Holiday Jokes
The World's Best Acting Jokes
The World's Best Drinking Jokes
More of the World's Best Drinking Jokes
The World's Best Gardening Jokes
The World's Best Motoring Jokes
The World's Best Gambling Jokes
The World's Best Marriage Jokes
The World's Best After-Dinner Jokes

The World's Best Skiing Jokes

Ernest Forbes

Cartoons by Graham Morris

HarperCollins*Publishers*

HarperCollins*Publishers*
77–85 Fulham Palace Road,
Hammersmith, London W6 8JB

A Paperback Original 1993
1 3 5 7 9 8 6 4 2

Copyright © Ernest Forbes 1993
Illustrations copyright © Graham Morris 1993

The Author asserts the moral right to
be identified as the author of this work

A catalogue record for this book
is available from the British Library

ISBN 0 00 638246 0

Set in Goudy Old Style by
Avocet Typesetters, Bicester, Oxon

Printed in Great Britain by
HarperCollinsManufacturing Glasgow

Author's Note

Had it been intended that man should ski — when I say man
I use it collectively to embrace all members of the human race
and politicians — we would have been born with feet which
grew lengthways to equal our height.

Skiing is definitely for the birds.

I'm glad I haven't to ski until tomorrow.

It is alleged that tall persons make
better skiers and this book is guaranteed
to increase your height . . .

. . . if you stand on it!

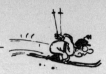

'Why the hell did you write that insurance policy for a 96-year-old man going on a skiing holiday?' shouted the manager at the travel clerk.

'Well,' said the clerk, 'I checked the records and no one of that age has ever had a skiing accident.'

The skier came to a stop at the end of the run and threw his poles, hat and gloves to the ground as he snorted in disgust, 'I've never skied so badly before!'

'Oh,' probed an interested instructor, 'you mean to say you've skied before?'

'What the hell happened to Graham this afternoon when he was jumping?' asked Ken. 'He left the jump in a perfect position then all of a sudden he went to pieces. Arms and legs all over the place, then down with a thump.'

'Well,' answered Tim, shaking his head in disbelief, 'in the middle of the jump his mobile phone rang and the silly bugger tried to answer it!'

The sports shop had a large sign: '50 PER CENT OFF ALL SPORTING EQUIPMENT.'

A man walked into the shop and, indicating the sign, asked the assistant, 'Does that apply to skis?'

'It does,' replied the assistant.

'Good,' acknowledged the man and took out his cheque-book, whereupon the assistant handed him one ski.

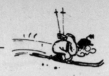

'My instructor says I would be a great skier except for two things,' announced a woman to her companion. 'Oh,' said the other woman, 'what are they?'

'My feet,' came the reply.

The ski instructress was talking to a class of beginners and explaining to them the various signs they would encounter in the sport.

'Signs at present are not universal,' pointed out the instructress. 'The colours and shapes of the signs are different in America, Europe and Australia. Some places have square signs, some diamond-shaped, some circles and some use balls. The only common factor is the colour black and that indicates the most difficult runs. Now, from what I have said, could anyone tell me where I would find black circles?'

'In Europe,' replied one man.

'Very good,' nodded the instructress. 'Now, where would I find black diamonds?'

'America and Australia,' came a quick answer.

'Excellent,' approved the instructress. 'And where would I find black balls?'

'The West Indies Cricket Team?' chirped a little blonde at the front of the class.

Her legs ached, her arms ached, her back ached, her head ached, in fact she ached all over. She spent most of her time on the slopes picking herself up. Her skis were constantly entangled, one pointing east the other pointing west. She even took a tumble when she tried to get on a chair lift and almost impaled her husband.

As she slowly dragged herself into the hotel bedroom, she croaked to her husband, 'Tell me again, darling, what a wonderful time we're having. I keep forgetting!'

'I would ski only I don't want to break a promise,' boasted the big-headed one.

'I would ski only I don't want to break a leg,' stated the honest one.

'I gave up fishing for skiing,' said Richard, 'and I must say, I would rather ski than fish.'

'Ah, you would rather battle against the elements than a fish,' said Larry.

'No, not really. But when you talk about skiing you don't have to produce evidence of your expertise,' replied Richard.

A man told his wife he was going on a business trip for a week but he had actually booked a week at a ski resort. He flew out of the country and was soon signing the register at the hotel, eager to hire the ski equipment and get on the slopes.

Properly equipped, he was enjoying the feeling of freedom and the crisp clear air when he suddenly realized he was lost. As he stared round him to get his bearings a huge hairy figure appeared, causing him to topple over and cry, 'Oh , Christ!'

'Please don't be afraid,' said the large figure in a soft voice. 'I am a yeti and I will not harm you.'

'Oh, it's not that I'm afraid of you,' replied the skier

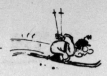

scrambling to his feet. 'But for a moment I thought you were my wife!'

The husband and wife were enjoying the skiing until the man suddenly lost control and went waist deep into the snow.

As he struggled to free himself his wife said, 'Hurry up, my feet are freezing.'

'You should be so lucky,' shuddered the husband.

The weather had suddenly turned bad and a snowstorm swirled up, restricting visibility. Members of the ski patrol were trying to check that there were no skiers out when a man almost skied into their office.

'You'll have to go and rescue my wife, she's trapped on the slope,' gasped the man as he started to remove his skis.

'Don't take off your skis,' said a member of the ski patrol. 'You can lead us to where you last saw her.'

'Are you mad?' yelled the skier. 'You don't really expect me to go out in weather like this?'

An Irishman and his wife arrived in Aspen, Colorado, for a skiing holiday and as they sat in the restaurant for their first meal the husband scanned the menu and asked his wife, 'What do you call that American dish I'm so wild about?'

'Goldie Hawn,' replied his wife without looking up from the menu.

The skier was making his way to the chair lift when he was stopped by a young woman.

'Good morning, sir,' greeted the young woman. 'My name is Barbara and I am carrying out a survey on behalf of the ski association as to the reason you chose this particular resort. I won't take up much of your time if you would be good enough to answer a few questions.'

'Certainly,' said the skier, resting on his poles.

'Thank you,' replied Barbara, holding her pen at the ready over her clipboard. 'Did you choose this resort because of the excellent skiing facilities?'

'No,' answered the young man.

'Because of the great training programme?'

'No.'

'Because you're sure to have good quality snow here?'

'No.'

'Because you are encouraged to take part in so many events?'

'No.'

'Because you can see so many world-class skiers here?'

'No.'

'Because of the wonderful hotel accommodation?'

'No.'

'Because of the world-famous food?'

'No.'

'Because some of the streets are heated and you can walk to the shops in comfort?'

'No.'

'Because of the shows in the evening?'

'No.'

'Well,' challenged the girl, 'why did you come here?'

'I won it in a holiday competition,' grinned the young man as he side-slipped away.

The ambulance men rushed the stretcher into the hospital. The injured man was lying face down on the stretcher with a ski pole sticking in his backside.

'What happened?' asked the doctor.

'Two skiers crashed into each other and in the tangle this man was impaled on the ski pole. We thought it would be better to leave it there until you saw it,' answered the ambulance man.

'Right,' said the doctor. 'Who is the man holding his hand?'

'That's the man who caused the injury.'

'He's showing a lot of concern,' commented the doctor.

'Not really,' replied the ambulance man. 'He wants his ski pole back!'

At the recent Winter Olympics the Irish downhill champion broke his leg in two places: once at the top of the run and once at the bottom.

Very early one morning at a ski resort a beginner went out to practise a few moves on his own without any onlookers. He was making slow and shaky progress when suddenly he was struck by a piste basher.

As he lay in hospital, legs in plaster, arms and head bandaged, one of his friends called to see him.

'You know,' advised his friend, 'you should sue for damages.'

'I don't want damages,' replied the injured skier. 'I want repairs!'

The ski instructor was talking to a class of beginners and was giving them a history of skiing.

'The "Hoting Ski", which was found in Sweden, is believed to be over four thousand years old,' explained the instructor. 'It is generally accepted that this ski was mainly used for hunting but sport has not been ruled out. I imagine any sport in which they would have taken part would have been very different from what we know today. Tell me, can anyone suggest two other ancient sports?'

'Certainly,' answered one would-be skier. 'Antony and Cleopatra?'

A doctor was explaining his surgery methods to his new assistant.

'When a young person comes to the surgery and is suffering from stress, I ask if he or she skis. If the answer is "yes", I advise them to stop at once. If the answer is "no", I advise them to start as soon as possible.'

'I believe you had a terrible fall,' observed a concerned skier when he met his friend.

'Indeed I did. Someone stole my skis,' came the sad reply.

'Stole your skis? Then how did you fall?' queried the puzzled man.

'They stole them while I was in the middle of a jump!'

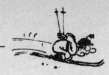

'Is it true you had glass skis made for your wife?' asked Alan.

'Quite true,' answered Tony.

'Glass skis? But why glass?' questioned Alan.

'So when she knocks someone down and skis over them, she'll see who it is!'

The two girls arrived at the resort for their first skiing holiday. They had a lot of luggage and immediately started to unpack when they reached their hotel room.

New ski suits, gloves, hats, boots, goggles, underclothes, soft boots, dresses, blouses, skirts, sweaters, shoes, coats, sun cream, lip salve, cameras, a video on skiing and make-up soon covered the bed.

As they stood looking at the collection of clothing and various other items one girl suddenly exclaimed, 'Oh, bother! We've forgotten to bring our skis!'

Desmond was enjoying his cross-country run when he heard the shouts and screams of a girl. He immediately headed in the direction of the cries. When he reached the scene he saw a girl lying on the ground and a man trying to stick her skis in the snow in the shape of a cross.

'What's happening?' shouted Desmond.

'This girl has had an accident and I'm marking the spot with her skis,' replied the man.

'You stupid bugger,' cried Desmond. 'You're supposed to take them off first!'

'Oh, I'm so thrilled,' cried the girl. 'My husband has just broken the record for the Irish ski jump. Has your husband broken anything in skiing?'

'He most certainly has,' answered the second girl. 'His collarbone, his right arm, both his legs and his left wrist!'

'Hello, George,' greeted David as he met his friend. 'Were you on the piste this afternoon?'

'Afraid not. Haven't had a drink since last night,' replied George.

A skier came off the jump and executed a long and graceful flight through the air, only to land slightly short of the leader.

'Dammit!' he snorted in anger. 'If only I'd farted harder.'

'Why didn't your husband join us?' asked one skier as Joan met up with the group.

'Oh, when he heard it was a dry slope he didn't want to come as he thought he wouldn't get a drink,' replied Joan.

The two bystanders watched as the world-famous cricketer, David Gower, completed the slalom course.

'He's not a bad skier,' commented one man.

'Not as good a skier as he is a cricketer,' countered the second man.

'Ah, but that's a completely different ball game,' defended the first man.

The girl very gingerly made her way to the nursery slope, taking her time to avoid a false move.

'Good morning,' said an instructor. 'This is a new experience for you, isn't it?'

'Yes, indeed it is,' replied the girl.

'Would I be right in saying that this was your very first time to ski?' asked the instructor.

'You would be quite right,' answered the girl. 'How did you know it was my first time?'

'You have your skis on back to front,' smiled the instructor.

The two women met in the gift shop at a ski resort and one greeted the other. 'Hello, Mary, I hear your husband had an accident and is in hospital.'

'Yes, he went off pissed and took a tumble,' replied the wife.

'You mean "off-piste"?'

'Oh no, I don't.'

The two men were enjoying their first skiing holiday and even managed to get a little skiing between bouts of drinking. They had arranged to meet in the bar for a pre-lunch drink and one man had already downed a couple of drinks before his friend arrived.

'What kept you?' enquired the tippler. 'You're already two drinks behind.'

'I was on that far run and some stupid bugger had stuck a lot of flags in the ground so I had to take them all out before I got going,' replied his friend.

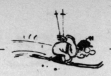

A prostitute went on a skiing holiday and was receiving her first lesson on the nursery slope. The instructor was showing her the stance

'Be relaxed, feet slightly apart for good balance, weight evenly distributed on both skis, bending a little forward from the waist. That's it, except for your legs, you'll never get anywhere with your legs so far apart.'

'Oh, I don't know,' replied the prostitute. 'I got on this holiday.'

The skier came off the jump and nose-dived into the ground, a tangle of arms, legs and skis.

'Hell!' said one skier standing at the ramp. 'Look at that!'

'Well,' said another skier, 'you shouldn't have pushed him when he said he had vertigo.'

'Vertigo!' exclaimed the first skier. 'Christ! I thought he said "Here we go"!'

'Mummy, may I go skiing?' asked the little girl.

'No, you may not, it's too dangerous,' replied her mother.

'But Daddy goes skiing,' persisted the little girl.

'Yes, but he's insured.'

'There's one thing I like about skiing as a sport,' observed the gentleman, fingering his MCC tie.

'What's that?' asked his companion.

'You're never bothered by a confounded streaker spoiling a run,' barked the gent.

A skier on his own on a cross-country run was travelling too fast when he realized he was heading for a gorge. In panic he drove his poles into the ground but only one pole took grip and he clung to it with both hands as he dangled over a 2,000-foot drop.

'Help! Help!' cried the terrified skier. 'Is there anyone up there? Help! Help!'

Afraid to move too much in case he dislodged the pole, he could already feel the cold creeping into his body.

'Help! Help!' he shouted again. 'Is there anyone up there?'

Suddenly a deep voice boomed across the sky, 'You will be saved, my son, if you will do as I say.'

The skier looked up but saw nothing but sky.

Again the voice boomed. 'Do as I say and you will be saved. Do you hear me?'

The now very cold skier answered, 'Yes, I hear you and I will do as you say.'

'Then let go of your ski pole and you will be saved,' commanded the voice.

The skier looked down at the frightening drop then, looking up, cried, 'Help! Help! Is there anyone ELSE up there?'

'My dog can ski.'
'He must be a very clever dog.'
'Oh, I don't know. He's fine on the jump but he stops at every gate on the slalom.'

Sign outside gents' toilet at a well-known ski resort:

PLEASE REMOVE SKIS BEFORE USING URINALS.

The two skiers were waiting for a T-bar lift and one remarked, 'Does it worry you that you could get injured skiing?'

'Not at all,' replied his companion cheerfully. 'Plenty of help available. There are usually more doctors on the slopes than in the hospitals.'

A bus-load of Irish tourists arrived in Aspen, Colorado, and the tour guide was telling them about the ski resort. 'Some of the streets in Aspen have underground heating so they are clear at all times,' she concluded.

'It's a pity they haven't got underground heating up those mountains to get rid of all that bloody snow,' remarked one tourist.

The man went into a shop selling sporting equipment and asked for a ski mask.

'Yes, sir,' said the assistant. 'Will there be anything else? Gloves? Boots? Poles? Helmet?'

'No, I don't need anything else to hold up a bank,' replied the man.

Skiing is like a career in politics. It takes you a long time to reach the top but you can come down in a few minutes.

The Englishman and the Irishman met on the nursery slope in a ski resort in Austria. 'Hello, Paddy,' greeted

the Englishman. 'I didn't expect to meet you here. The last I heard from you was that you wanted to water ski.'

'I did,' replied Paddy, 'but I couldn't find a lake with a slope.'

'I believe your husband had a nasty fall on your skiing holiday,' said Anna to her friend Linda.

'Indeed he did,' replied Linda without much sympathy.

'Did he fall off the jump or the run?' asked Anna.

'The barstool,' came the curt reply.

The girl reached the end of the run and said to her instructor, 'I love skiing. I could ski like this for ever.'

'Oh,' said the instructor, 'you mean you don't want to improve?'

The two women were having a little gossip about their hostess, who was out of the room.

'She's a very sporting type,' said one. 'Called her second son Ski because she's so fond of skiing.'

'Oh,' remarked the other woman, 'I wondered why she called her first son Dick.'

'Did you enjoy your skiing holiday,' enquired Joan.

'Oh yes, it was wonderful,' enthused Jean.

'And what about your husband? Has he improved since you taught him to ski last year?' went on Joan.

'Indeed he has improved,' exclaimed Jean. 'This year he only broke one leg.'

'What do you get if you cross one ski with another ski?' asked Charles.

'I don't know. What do you get if you cross one ski with another ski?' queried Andy.

'A bloody broken leg,' replied Charles.

Sir Anthony Hopkins, the Oscar-winning actor, went on a skiing holiday to Switzerland and one day he went for a cross-country trek alone. He was enjoying the solitude and possibly thinking of winning another Oscar when he hit an icy patch and fell, injuring his ankle. He was unable to put any weight on his foot so skiing and walking were both out of the question. He knew he couldn't crawl the distance in the snow and was pondering on his next action when a St Bernard rescue dog trotted up beside him and licked his face. Sir Anthony heaved himself on to the back of the dog, which set off in a homeward direction.

Suddenly the weather deteriorated, a snowstorm broke and visibility was nil, yet the dog struggled on through the snow. Eventually Sir Anthony spotted a light and guided the dog to it.

When they finally reached the light, which was coming from a lodge, both the actor and the dog were exhausted. Sir Anthony knocked loudly on the door, which was opened by a hatchet-faced woman.

'What do you want?' she asked in an unpleasant voice.

'We need help, madam. Look, this poor dog is completely exhausted, he has carried me for miles. I have an injured ankle and we haven't eaten or had anything to drink for hours,' gasped Sir Anthony.

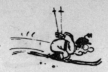

'Well, you can't stay here,' snarled the woman. 'This lodge is for women only.'

'But surely, madam, surely,' pleaded Sir Anthony, 'you wouldn't turn a knight out on a dog like this?'

The girl was about to make her first ski jump and was feeling very apprehensive. 'Are you sure', she asked her instructor, 'that I'm ready to make this jump?'

'I wouldn't let you try the jump if I didn't think you could do it,' replied the instructor with a confident smile.

'I hope you're right,' replied the girl nervously.

'Of course I'm right,' assured the instructor. 'Just what is worrying you?'

'It's just that period in the air, after I jump and before I land,' said the girl. 'Sort of suspended in midair.'

'Don't worry about that,' encouraged the instructor, patting the girl's shoulder. 'I've never left anyone up there yet.'

The man was lying in a hospital bed, completely swathed in bandages and plaster. A doctor was standing beside the bed filling in a chart when a man walked in to the ward.

'May I speak to Eric, doctor?' asked the visitor.

'Who are you?' asked the doctor.

'I'm his skiing companion. I was with him when he had the accident.'

'Is it important?'

'Well, it is bad news,' replied the man.

'You're telling me', exclaimed the doctor, 'that you have

bad news for a man who has broken practically every bone in his body?'

'Yes, he broke his skis as well!'

The two girls were discussing skiing and how much they would like to go to a ski resort when their aunt overheard them.

'Girls,' warned their aunt, 'you must be very careful if you go skiing. Some years ago I went skiing and injured myself so badly I could never ski again.'

'Oh, that was terrible,' said one girl.

'Indeed it was,' agreed the other girl, tugging her ear thoughtfully. 'Tell me, Auntie, what did you do with your skis?'

'Darling,' shouted Rodney as he charged into the house, 'I have just been speaking to Fred and he suggested we should have another skiing holiday like last year; the four of us, you, Jill, Fred and me. What do you think?'

'No!' screeched his wife. 'After last year and that disgusting episode I'll never go skiing with you again. Can you imagine the humiliation and embarrassment Jill and I felt when you and Fred decided to have a pee on the top of the mountain and we had to get the Red Cross to force you apart?'

At the shopping complex in the ski resort the two Englishwomen met as they examined the range of goods. After some general conversation one woman remarked, 'I

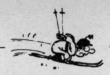

thought I'd do some shopping today for a change. Skiing every day can be quite tiring, don't you think?'

'I wouldn't know, I haven't skied since I arrived and I don't intend starting to ski,' replied the second woman.

'But why come to a ski resort if you don't want to ski?' asked the first woman in surprise.

'It was all a mistake,' answered the second woman. 'My husband asked me if I would like to go on a biathlon holiday and I thought biathlon was in Africa!'

The injured skier lay in a hospital bed covered from head to foot in bandages. His tearful wife sat by his bedside.

'What happened to Graham?' asked a visiting friend.

As the man couldn't speak his wife answered. 'Oh, dear, it was all my fault. As you know, Graham is a television engineer, so the other day when they asked if anyone would like to have a go at the aerials I submitted Graham's name.'

The two Irishmen listened attentively to the ski instructor who had just remarked that a ski should be well tuned. 'Somebody should tell that man it's a ski I have here, not a bloody piano,' grunted one Irishman.

The Englishman and his wife were enjoying their skiing holiday in Austria when a group arrived from England. The group was comprised of middle-aged men and a couple

of ladies of the same vintage and all the members of the group really lived it up, après-ski being high on the list.

One night in the bar the Englishman nodded towards the fun-making group and said, 'They really enjoy themselves but I haven't seen any of them actually skiing. Any idea if they belong to a ski club?'

'Oh, no,' informed his wife, 'they're not here to ski, they are all councillors on the Bradtown City Council and they're on a fact-finding trip.'

'I didn't think they would consider opening a ski resort anywhere near Bradtown,' said the Englishman, 'it doesn't seem a suitable location.'

'Oh, it's not to open a ski resort,' corrected his wife. 'Some man wants to sell ski equipment at his market stall and the council need to know what's involved!'

The married couple, skiing in France, had gone off-piste and soon were separated. The husband skied swiftly and soon left his wife far behind, but she was quite content to ski at her own speed and enjoy the surroundings. She was happily pottering along when a member of the ski patrol hailed her.

'Oh, Mrs Tibbs, I have some bad news for you. Your husband fell into a crevasse and we are trying to get him out,' informed the patrolman.

'Oh, dear!' cried Mrs Tibbs, putting her hand to her mouth.

'Please don't distress yourself,' comforted the ski patrol member. 'We are doing our best to rescue him.'

'I'm sure you are,' said the upset Mrs Tibbs. 'It's just that he's got the key of the hotel room in his pocket!'

The two women were having a telephone conversation and one remarked, 'My husband has gone out tonight. He's playing in a snooker competition.'

'My husband is also out,' said the second woman. 'He has gone to a skiing class at the local school hall.'

'I didn't know they taught skiing at the local school hall,' commented the first woman.

'Well, they don't actually teach you how to ski, just how to fill out your accident claim forms,' advised the second woman.

It was après-ski time and the two married couples were discussing the events of the day.

'We had a lovely day,' said Paul. 'Kim's a great skier, but she will keep stopping to admire the beauty of it all.'

'I know,' agreed Kim. 'When you are so high up the mountain it's so beautiful and peaceful.'

'Yes,' cut in Vera, 'it's all just like a winter wonderland.'

'Wonderland is right,' grunted Barry. 'When Vera jumps I wonder where the hell she'll land.'

The senior ski instructor at Aspen beckoned to the new instructor and warned, 'Look son, when you take a class of ladies you refer to them as that – a class of ladies – not chicks on sticks!'

Olive and Jean met in a supermarket and Olive said in a consoling voice, 'Oh, my dear. I believe you lost your husband.'

Jean nodded her head in reply.

'Oh, I'm so sorry,' went on Olive. 'How did it happen?'

'Skiing,' replied Jean.

'Skiing,' repeated Olive sadly, shaking her head. 'Was it a terrible accident?'

'No accident at all,' snapped Jean. 'He ran off with a little blonde he met on the slopes at Aspen!'

'I love skiing,' remarked Bob. 'Why don't you try it, Johnny?'

'Skiing? Not on your life,' observed Johnny, shaking his head. 'Flying hundreds of feet in the air and hurtling down steep hills at excessive speed is absolutely ridiculous. There must be easier ways of meeting nurses.'

It was après-ski time and the drink and the tall stories were flowing freely. The alleged skill of the skiers was amazing and only one middle-aged man sat quietly, smoking his pipe, enjoying his drink and listening to the tales of skiing expertise. One member of the crowd turned to him and asked, 'What about your skiing skills, Harry?'

'No skiing skills,' replied Harry. 'I'm a ski bum.'

'You're not a ski bum,' laughed another member of the party.

'Indeed I am,' nodded Harry. 'All you people come to ski, I come to look at the pretty girls and their lovely bums when they are skiing.'

The ski patrol was alerted that an intoxicated man had gone off-piste and other skiers were concerned for his

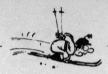

safety. A member of the ski patrol set off to search but had no difficulty finding the lost skier as he was propped on his ski poles drinking from a hip flask.

'Come along, sir,' said the ski patrol member, 'I'll guide you back.'

'Why should you guide me back?' queried the unsteady skier.

'Because you're lost and you're drunk,' came the blunt reply.

'I most certainly am not drunk,' slurred the man, 'and I am only lost because the weather deteriorated so quickly that I couldn't see the tips of my four skis!'

The ski instructor was very enthusiastic about skiing and got quite carried away as he told the mixed class: 'Skiing is like having sex, it has all the thrill of sex, it has all the excitement of sex, it has all the pleasure of sex, it has all the fulfilment of sex, it has all the rapture of sex, it has all the ecstasy of sex and it has all the delight of sex.'

'Then why the hell don't we partner off and go to bed and have sex?' piped up one man. 'It would be a lot bloody warmer!'

The team manager was berating a skier for coming third in a race.

'You should have won that race,' rebuked the manager. 'At the final turn I saw that hole opening up between the two leaders. Why didn't you go through it?'

'Bloody hell!' shouted the skier. 'Have you ever tried to ski through a hole that was moving faster than you?'

'Where did you and your husband go on holiday this year?' a woman asked her friend.

'We went to Val Thorens on a skiing holiday. It was really wonderful,' replied the second woman.

'Where is Val Thorens?' enquired the first woman. 'I've never heard of it.'

'I don't know where it is,' answered the woman. 'We flew.'

A ski instructor was talking to a pretty girl when she suddenly drew back and slapped his face. So hard was the slap that the man went sprawling in the snow as the girl stalked away.

Another ski instructor went over to give his colleague a helping hand and asked, 'What on earth did you say to her?'

'I don't know,' answered the ski instructor rubbing his face. 'As far as I was concerned we were talking about ski boots and I asked her if she preferred a front or rear entry and the next thing — wham!'

The two former skiers watched a skier wobbling as he made his landing.

'Vandermann just isn't championship class,' pointed out one ex-skier.

'Yes, but you couldn't tell him that, he thinks he's the best. A household name in skiing,' said the second ex-skier, shaking a finger.

'Household name in skiing!' exclaimed the other man. 'Why, he's not even a household name in his own household!'

'When I spoke to you yesterday I told you to try and get the "feel" of the slope. Did anyone take my advice?' the ski instructor asked the class.

'I certainly did,' replied a pretty blonde, 'and I have the bruises to prove it.'

'Sudden deceleration', pointed out the instructor as he helped the skier to his feet, 'does not mean you ski directly into a tree.'

The man and the girl on a skiing holiday in Austria went off-piste and far in the distance spotted an old castle on a mountain top.

'That reminds me of that film . . . oh, what is the name of it?' struggled the girl.

'Colditz?' suggested the man helpfully.

'No,' replied the girl, 'I'm wearing a padded bra.'

'Well,' said the ski instructor, 'this is the big test, your first jump. How do you feel?'

'Rather like a turkey as Christmas draws near,' croaked the apprehensive skier.

A group of boys went on a skiing holiday and at the ski resort they met some girls from a club near their home town.

One girl from the club prided herself on being a good sport and demonstrated this by accepting every skiing challenge

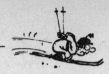

from the boys, moguls, off-piste, slalom or jumps. She soon had the nickname of Good Sport.

Good Sport and Bob, one of the boys of the group, also enjoyed a few evenings together.

Holiday over, Bob had almost forgotten it when, a couple of months later, his telephone rang.

'Do you know who this is?' asked a sweet feminine voice. Bob hadn't a clue.

'This is Good Sport,' went on the voice. 'I need to see you, it's very important. When can we meet?'

They met for lunch that day and after recalling some memories of the skiing holiday the girl blurted out that she was pregnant and asked Bob what he was going to do about it.

'I don't know what I can do,' gulped Bob. 'That holiday was just for fun. I'm engaged to another girl and we're soon to get married. The question is what are you going to do about it?'

'Well,' said the girl tearfully, 'I suppose I could kill myself!'

'By jove!' breathed Bob. 'Now I know why we nicknamed you Good Sport. You really are a good sport!'

The girl stood looking up at the mountains and the brightly clad skiers on the runs. She turned quickly and her skis, which were resting on her shoulders, hit a man and knocked him down.

'Oh, I'm so sorry,' apologized the girl.

'That's all right,' replied the man, struggling to his feet.

'I've never skied before and I was wondering if it mattered which run I tried first,' said the girl watching the speeding skiers on the black run.

'Not to me it doesn't,' muttered the man, tenderly rubbing his head.

The two girls were giving the ski instructor a rough time with their non-stop questioning.

'What should we do', asked one girl, 'if we are out skiing and see an avalanche coming our way?'

'Turn and ski away from it,' advised the instructor.

'Is that all?' questioned the second girl.

'Not quite, you also have to travel faster than the avalanche,' pointed out the instructor.

At an infants' school in Aspen, Colorado, the visiting preacher was talking to a class of young children about Heaven.

'All the children who would like to go to Heaven raise their hands,' said the preacher.

Only one boy in the front didn't raise his hand.

'Would you not like to go to Heaven?' asked the preacher, addressing the little boy.

'Sure I'd like to go Heaven, but I can't,' answered the little boy. 'I've got ski practice at two-thirty.'

It's not a sin to ski on a Sunday but the way some people ski it's a bloody crime!

'My son won a prize in a fishing competition in Gstaad,' said the proud mother.

'Oh, I thought Gstaad was a ski resort,' commented her friend.

'So did I,' agreed the mother, 'but on a postcard he sent me he wrote that he had won a giant salmon.'

I was watching you on the nursery slope this morning,' said the young man as he handed the girl a drink.

'Oh, I've been paying for extra lessons for ten days so I'm getting used to the slope,' replied the girl.

'I must introduce you to my brother,' suggested the young man. 'Perhaps he could help you.'

'Is he a ski instructor?' asked the girl.

'No, a solicitor. He may be able to get your money back.'

The vicar called at the home of one of his parishioners and as the husband, whom he had wanted to see, wasn't in he spoke to the wife.

'I have heard that Philip is in the habit of going over to the ski club on a Sunday morning,' said the vicar in a severe voice as he interlocked his fingers.

'Oh, but he doesn't go to ski. He only goes for a drink and a chat with the boys,' said the helpful wife.

The blonde Irish girl was trying to find the connection between skiing and music.

'Why should there be a connection?' asked her friend.

'Well, every time my husband goes out to ski he's as fit as a fiddle and when he returns he's as tight as a drum,' explained the blonde.

'Did you hear the terrible news about Ted Scott?' asked one skier as he examined the edge of his ski.

'No, what happened?' enquired his fellow skier.

'He came out on Monday morning to ski and on his way to the chair lift he tripped and injured his ankle and had to return to his hotel. When he got to his room he found his wife in bed with a man! Shot both of them!'

'Could have been worse.'

'Worse? What do you mean?' queried the first skier.

'Well,' answered the second skier, 'if he had injured his ankle on Saturday morning he would have bloody well shot me!'

Two members of the ski patrol sped after a skier who was skiing in a most erratic fashion. They caught the man, only to find he was so drunk he could hardly stand. How he managed to ski was a complete mystery.

'Sir, you are in no fit condition to ski, we will escort you back to your hotel,' said one member of the ski patrol firmly.

'And you'll tell my wife,' beamed the happy skier.

'Tell her what? asked the official.

'Tell her it is not a good idea to get drunk before you go to ski,' gurgled the man.

'Of course you shouldn't drink and ski,' ordered the patrolman. 'But why should I tell your wife?'

'Because she was the one who suggested it,' came the head-shaking reply.

'Are you sure she told you to drink before you went skiing?' queried the doubtful patrol member.

'Of course I'm sure,' answered the inebriated spouse. 'She told me this morning if I was going skiing I should go off-pissed so I took her at her word!'

The British politician was checking into the hotel at a ski resort in Switzerland when he spotted a suite called the British Royal Family Suite. Pointing at the notice, he said to the reception manager, 'I say, that's a bit thick. A member of our Royal Family stays once at your hotel and you have the audacity to name the suite the British Royal Family Suite!'

'Stayed once!' exclaimed the manager. 'Sir, the suite is always occupied!'

Bill had gone skiing alone as his wife complained of a headache and remained in the hotel bedroom. He went off-piste and was enjoying the scenery when he heard a cry for help. He yelled back and skied in the direction of the shouts to arrive at a very steep drop and there found a man dangling from the cliff, holding on to one ski pole which had jammed between rocks. Releasing his skis and throwing off his ski poles, Bill crawled to a position where he could reach the man's arm. Noting the man had already kicked off his skis, Bill suggested he get rid of the free ski pole so as not to impede the rescue.

'No, no, I can't,' gasped the man. 'I must keep my ski poles.'

'Oh, if you must,' grunted Bill, not having time to argue.

After considerable hauling and heaving the man was pulled to safety.

'Thank you,' said the man. 'I owe you my life, my friend.'

'Glad I could help,' shrugged Bill. 'But tell me, why are your ski poles so important that you wouldn't part with them?'

The man lay silent for a moment then said, 'Well, I suppose I owe you an explanation considering you saved my life. I am a professional assassin and these ski poles connect together to make a high-powered rifle with telescopic sight. Look, I'll show you.'

As he spoke, the assassin connected the ski poles to make a rifle then handed it to Bill. 'Look through the sight and you'll see how good it is.'

'That is wonderful!' exclaimed Bill as he looked through the sight. 'I can see my hotel quite clearly and there is my window. Christ! That's my wife and Robin Willis is with her and they are both naked and making love. That bastard! Bloody headache indeed! Look, I'll give you £5,000 if you shoot my wife in the head!'

The assassin held his hand up in rejection.

'Please,' pleaded Bill. 'After all, just think what that woman is doing to me. And I'll give you another £5,000 if you shoot his dick off!'

'Well,' said the assassin slowly, 'I do owe you a favour.' He began to position himself and line up his target.

'Hurry up, hurry up,' urged Bill, full of rage.

'Easy my friend, easy,' whispered the assassin. 'I'm just trying to save you £5,000!'

'Are you going skiing this year?' asked Rose.

'Oh yes, as far as Larry is concerned he hasn't had a holiday unless he's been skiing. He's already preparing for it and we don't go for four months,' answered Norma.

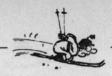

'Preparing for a skiing holiday?' questioned Rose. 'What preparation is there?'

'Well, Larry maintains that skiing makes you use muscles you didn't know you had so you must be very fit. He runs six miles a day, then has a work-out, never uses a lift or escalator, runs up steps and stairs two steps at a time. Never uses the car if he can walk, if he uses a bus he gets off two stops before he needs to and walks the rest, plays squash four times a week, does special exercises to strengthen his arms, wears his ski boots as often as possible to get his feet and ankles used to them and has spring grips to carry out wrist exercises. What exercises does your husband do?'

'The only exercise he gets is nocturnal, horizontal and too bloody quick!' complained Rose.

The two Irishmen were on a skiing holiday and one day they went on a cross-country run without a guide and were happily skiing around when they suddenly came across some huge footprints.

'He must have been a helluva size to make prints like that,' pointed out Paddy.

'And barefooted at that,' remarked Sean.

'Do you think it is a yeti?' questioned Paddy.

'Boy, if it is this is a wonderful chance to find him,' Sean eagerly responded.

'You're right there,' agreed Paddy. 'So I'll tell you what we'll do, you follow the prints to see where he went and I'll backtrack to see where he came from!'

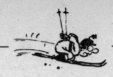

The husband stormed into the house and started to pack a suitcase.

'What are you doing?' asked his wife.

'The pressure of it all is too much for me,' cried the husband. 'I want to get away from it all, to feel the cold crisp wind on my cheeks, the crunch of virgin snow, the clear starry nights, that special breeze as you speed downhill and, above all, that indescribable silence at the top of the mountain. I'm going skiing and I warn you! Don't try to stop me!'

'Try to stop you!' cried the wife. 'Who is trying to stop you? I'm coming with you!'

The manager was retiring from the firm at the age of sixty and the staff presented him with skis as a retirement present.

'How very kind,' exclaimed his wife. 'They knew you had enjoyed your skiing holiday.'

'But that was years ago,' said the husband with some doubt. 'At my age I'm not sure if this gift is one of appreciation or revenge!'

'My wife and I both love a white Christmas,' said the husband. 'Only trouble is, I think of skiing, she thinks of ermine and mink.'

The first-time skier was booking into his hotel at the ski resort. As he signed the register he indicated the last column and asked the hotel clerk, 'What do I fill in here?'

'Your blood group,' replied the clerk.

'I cannot understand that woman, Barbara Russell,' stormed Mrs Manders. 'This is a selective ski resort and she is wearing those brightly coloured clothes. Why, they are practically fluorescent.'

'That's so she can be easily seen,' explained her husband.

'What!' thundered Mrs Manders. 'In the bar?'

The American husband arrived home with new ski equipment, skis, boots, poles, clothes, the lot.

'What are you doing with that stuff?' demanded his wife.

'I bought it,' replied her husband.

'Bought it?' shouted his wife. 'What for?'

'Well, sweetie, you remember you told me to call in the general store and get a packet of Tampax? Well, when I called at the store and told the girl what I wanted and that we were going to Aspen for the weekend she said she hoped I enjoyed the skiing but I told her I didn't ski.'

'So why this lot?' persisted the wife.

'Well, when the girl heard I didn't ski she handed me the Tampax and said I was going to have a real boring weekend. So then she sold me the gear.'

The woman was not a natural skier. She couldn't even master the most basic movements and her instructor was slowly going mad. The woman, cheerfully unaware of his frustration, brightly requested, 'Do you mind if we finish a little earlier today? It's my husband's birthday and I want to get him a present. What do you think I should give him?'

'How about your skis?' suggested the weary instructor.

'I think Roger is skiing on his nerves,' remarked a team member to the team captain as they watched a skier competing in the giant slalom.

'Well, I wish to Christ he would just ski on the course,' grunted the captain.

'My wife says if I don't give up skiing she is going to leave me.'

'I'm sorry to hear that.'

'So am I. Means I'll have to find someone to feed the cat.'

The skier was lying face down in the snow. She was breathless, bruised, battered and very angry as the two male skiers stopped to assist her.

'Nasty fall,' observed one man.

'Fall my arse,' scolded the woman. 'I didn't fall! I was flattened by a raving madman and he didn't stop to see if I was injured.'

'Would you recognize him if you saw him?' enquired one man.

'I most certainly would,' snorted the lady, her breath almost melting the snow.

'Then you got a good look at him?' said one of the helpers.

'No, I didn't see him at all but I'd know that laugh anywhere,' growled the woman.

The young man thought he was an excellent skier and on his arrival at the ski resort he sought out the chief ski

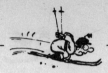

instructor to question him on the resort as well as to air his knowledge on skiing.

'What are your off-piste runs like?' asked the skier. 'I like runs that are completely ungroomed, preferably unskied, with the danger of an avalanche and that really offer a challenge.'

'Well,' affirmed the instructor, 'I think you'll find some of our off-piste runs a real challenge. Frankly, we don't advise skiers to go alone, they should always be accompanied by a member of our staff.'

'Wouldn't hear tell of it,' boasted the skier. 'The thrill is doing it on your own. Of course, you have a slalom?'

'Of course.'

'Giant slalom?'

'Yes, a giant slalom,' answered the instructor with polite weariness.

'What about a super giant slalom?' enthused the skier.

'No problem,' sighed the instructor.

'And moguls,' persisted the skier, 'are they rough?'

'Rough?' replied the instructor. 'You won't find rougher anywhere. Why, only last week there was a young skier who tried the mogul run, he went up as Mr Smith and by the time he had finished the run he was Miss Smith.'

The instructor was talking to a class of new arrivals on the basics of skiing.

'When you are going to turn, be gentle with your skis, don't try and push them around but slowly change the pressure on your skis by moving your body over the ski you want to turn.'

At this point the instructor paused and looking at a pretty girl of considerable bust proportions he rubbed his chin thoughtfully and continued, 'In your case, Miss, rather than risk overbalancing, I think it's always going to be schuss for you!'

A fellow was staying at a Scottish skiing, hunting, fishing and recreational resort and one day when out skiing he went so far off-piste he became completely lost. He went on a downhill track and landed head first in a snow drift. He was kicking his legs madly in the air when he heard the sound of gun shots and got the impression he was in the line of fire, so, releasing his skis, he grabbed them and wriggled along the ground until he came to a beaten path and eventually found his way back to the lodge.

That evening when the skier went into the bar at the hotel a large ex-major was telling the other drinkers of the large deer he had shot that afternoon. 'It had the most wonderful pair of antlers you could imagine, and he was clever, kept them moving all the time, but I bagged him! However, when I got to the spot where he must have fallen I could see the tracks in the snow where he had been dragged away by some bounder!'

The two girls scrambled on to the chair lift and one panted, 'Your husband is in a bad mood this morning. Is he suffering from the flight over last night?'

'No, he just found out that the T-bar wasn't a place to get a drink,' grunted the wife.

'My husband is completely useless,' complained the angry wife when she returned from a skiing holiday with her husband. 'He's the only person in the world I know to trip over the fall-line!'

A skier was skiing off-piste when he realized he was heading for a deep drop. He tried to stop but took a tumble, was knocked unconscious and slid over the cliff to land in soft snow.

The rescue party arrived and had him on a stretcher and were carrying him away when he recovered consciousness. His hand slid off the stretcher and he felt nothing but air.

'Christ!' he exclaimed without opening his eyes. 'I haven't hit the ground yet!'

'What did the doctor say after examining your husband?' asked June.

'Oh dear, that's a very sore subject with George,' answered Jean. 'The doctor told him to get a lot more exercise.'

'But he has just returned from a two-week skiing holiday with the Former Pupils Association. Surely he got all the exercise he needed when he was away,' pointed out June.

'Well, it appears that the doctor is also a former pupil and was on the skiing trip and said that the only exercise George got was to his jaw and elbow,' confided Jean.

R oger was explaining to Paddy the joys of skiing, particularly skiing a mogul field. 'The thrill of the run,

the challenge of the valleys and bumps, your body swaying to the contours, the coldness against your face and the flush of achievement when you finish the run. It's wonderful!'

'A lot of nonsense,' argued the Irishman. 'If God had wanted us to ski he would have given us wings!'

Is your husband enjoying the skiing?' asked Mrs Foster as she climbed on to a chair lift with Mrs Mills.

'Oh, I'm afraid not,' replied Mrs Mills. 'I don't think John will ever be a skier. He spends so much time in deep snow, the instructor has issued him with a snorkel!'

The bride watched in puzzlement as the bridegroom packed his skis into the taxi, then asked, 'Barry, why are you taking your skis on our honeymoon?'

'Well, it's my first time in Switzerland and I'd like to have some fun when I'm there,' replied Barry.

Jackie thought she was a good skier on the slalom course and went to an agent regarding sponsorship.

'Oh, I don't know,' said the agent. 'I do have a brewery looking for a sporting personality but these people want the name of their product to be prominently displayed.'

'Well, I could have the name of the brewery on the back and front of my jacket and a band around my hat,' suggested Jackie.

'I don't think so,' murmured the agent, shaking his head. 'Sponsors demand a lot of exposure, unless . . .'

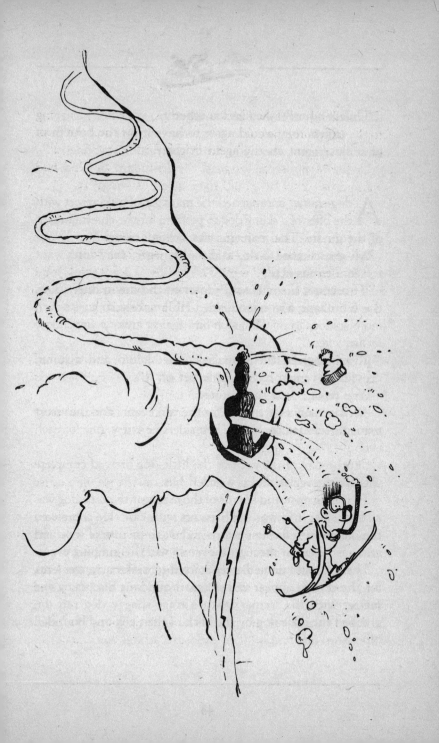

'Unless what?' asked Jackie eagerly.

'. . . unless they would agree to have it on the bottom of your skis,' went on the agent brightly.

A dog-trainer approached the manager of a ski resort with the offer of a skiing dog to perform for the entertainment of the guests. The manager was not impressed.

'My guests come to ski,' said the manager, 'they don't want to see a circus act.'

'This is not a circus act,' protested the dog-trainer. 'This dog is brilliant, a wonderful skier. He'll make your guests even more anxious to ski. I'll match him against anyone you choose in any event.'

'Right,' agreed the manager. 'The slalom and a jump, providing we can have a little bet on it.'

'You're on,' said the trainer.

Arrangements were made for the two events and the resort manager selected two of the best skiers he knew, one for each event.

On the day of the contest the little dog arrived complete with skis, goggles and a woollen hat.

To the surprise and horror of the manager the little dog was a super skier and won both events with ease. He completed the slalom with flawless action and was a picture of style and grace as he sailed through the air to win the jumping event.

The manager immediately started to make arrangements for the dog to appear at the resort and was discussing the matter with the trainer when a huge shaggy dog ran up, grabbed the little dog by the back of the neck and bounded off.

'What's all that about?' shouted the manager.

'Oh hell!' exclaimed the trainer in rage. 'That's his mother and she wants him to be a vet!'

'I see you still use a dog in your rescue operations,' remarked a skier, indicating a large dog.

'Indeed we do,' replied the member of the ski patrol. 'We also use helicopters, heat-seeking devices and other modern rescue equipment but this is a great fellow, never lets you down.'

'Why do you have two barrels strapped to his neck? Is it for easy conveyance?' enquired the skier.

'No,' replied the patrol officer, patting the dog, 'one barrel has brandy in it and the other has ginger ale, just in case the victim doesn't want his or her brandy straight.'

The four American ladies settled down to have their weekly coffee morning and news session.

'My son,' exclaimed one woman proudly,' has been made captain of his college football team.'

'That's nice,' said the second woman. 'My son has just had an offer to play baseball for the California Angels.'

'Isn't that great!' gushed the third woman. 'Well, I must tell you that my son has been selected to tour America to play basketball.'

The three proud mothers looked at the fourth woman.

'Well,' admitted the fourth woman, 'my son skis and I know nothing about the game. I don't even know what sort of ball they use.'

A doctor and his wife were returning to their hotel after a morning on the slopes. As they entered the lounge a very attractive blonde in a tight-fitting ski suit said hello to the doctor.

'And who was that?' questioned the wife.

'Oh, just a young woman I know professionally,' stammered the doctor going red.

'I'm sure of that,' said the wife, 'but your profession or hers?'

A group of British MPs was spending the Easter break at a ski resort in Switzerland and a couple of days after their arrival two of them were sitting in the bar having an afternoon drink. The manager of the hotel approached them and said, 'I'm sorry, gentlemen, to be the bearer of bad news, but I've just been told that a member of your party has been injured in a fall.'

'Who is it?' asked one MP as he and his companion rose.

'I don't know. I wasn't given a name,' replied the manager.

'Any idea what happened?'

'Apparently he misjudged the run, went over a cliff and fell two hundred feet,' advised the manager, sadly shaking his head.

'What about his injuries?' enquired one politician.

'It appears he landed on his head,' was the grave reply.

Both MPs sat down.

'Oh, that's all right then,' chirped one politician. 'No damage done!'

Heather was busy tidying up her office desk in readiness for her vacation which she was about to take.

'Any plans made for your holidays?' asked Dorothy, one of her female colleagues.

'Yes,' replied Heather, 'I'm going skiing and I'm really looking forward to it.'

'It sounds great,' said Dorothy. 'Where are you going?'

'A ski resort in Colorado,' beamed Heather.

'That's wonderful,' said Dorothy. 'Where in Colorado?'

'Frozen Hole Mountain,' informed Heather.

Dorothy paused for a moment before asking, 'Is that a location or a condition?'

Sue was horrified when she saw her husband, William, and another skier drop their ski poles and start throwing punches at each other.

She immediately ran to stop the fight shouting, 'William! Stop it! We'll talk about it!'

'There is nothing to talk about,' panted William, dodging a wild swing. 'He started it and I'm going to finish it.'

'I didn't start anything,' protested the other skier. 'I only asked him where he was going to ski and he told me to "piss off"!'

'Oh, William,' rebuked Sue, getting between the two men, 'I've told you a thousand times to be careful, you always get it the wrong way round!'

A vicar on a skiing holiday prepared for the giant slalom, he checked his gear and skis, said a silent prayer to the sky and set off. His performance was excellent. The following

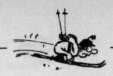

day he went through the same routine and once again gave a first-class performance. On the third day as he prepared for his run he was approached by another skier who observed, 'Vicar, I notice you always say a prayer before starting your run, do you think it would do me any good if I were to say a prayer?'

'Well,' said the vicar, adjusting his goggles, 'saying a prayer certainly won't do you any harm. Always worth a try.'

After a smile of approval, the vicar said his little prayer, set off and once again had a flawless run.

The other skier looked skyward, muttered a prayer and started his run. It was absolutely horrendous, unbelievably bad from start to finish and he was in a flaming mood when he tackled the vicar.

'So much for your bloody prayer,' stormed the skier, 'it didn't do me much good!'

'Ah,' smiled the vicar, 'as well as praying you also need to be able to ski well!'

Over an evening drink in the bar of the hotel at the ski resort the young man told the two girls he was a very accomplished skier.

The following morning the two girls were on the nursery slope and were very surprised when they came upon the young man lying face down in the snow, doing his best to struggle to his feet.

'Hello,' shouted one of the girls cheerfully. 'After what you told us last night I didn't think you would fall.'

'I didn't fall,' spluttered the young man as he spat out snow.

'What are you doing down there then?' laughed the girl.

'Checking the texture of the snow,' gasped the young man.

'That was another lovely jump,' applauded an observing official as the skier made a perfect landing. 'That's the third jump you've made at over eighty-seven metres. I don't suppose you'll try for a longer jump; you're probably quite happy with your pesent form. There's nothing else you need to prove.'

'Well there is one thing I'd like to do sometime,' said the skier.

'What's that?' asked the official.

'Make that jump with my eyes open,' replied the skier.

As Gerry and Des slipped off the T-bar lift and moved aside, Gerry remarked, 'I was sorry to hear about David.'

'What happened to David?' asked Des.

'He had a nervous breakdown,' replied Gerry.

'Oh, what caused that?' enquired Des. 'Pressure of work, domestic problems or just trying to make ends meet?'

'Nothing like that,' said Gerry. 'Skiing was his problem.'

'Skiing? How did skiing cause a nervous breakdown?' puzzled Des.

'Well you know how obsessed David was about his downhill racing,' went on Gerry.

'Yes, indeed,' nodded Des.

'Well the other day he started downhill, assumed the egg position and just cracked,' explained Gerry.

The skier overbalanced as he came off the jump and crashed to the ground. It was his last jump on earth and he found himself in the great ski resort in the sky. There he was greeted by St Peter. 'Ah Michael, right on time.'

'You mean you were expecting me?' asked Michael.

'Of course,' answered the saint.

'But if I had made a good jump I wouldn't be here,' pointed out Michael.

'You would have been here no matter what your jump was like,' intoned St Peter. 'And, after all, you are in Heaven. Would you like to see around?'

'Yes, I would,' answered the skier.

St Peter showed Michael Heaven and told him what his duties would be. During the tour Michael looked down and to his surprise saw ski slopes, ski jumps and a great slalom course.

'Where is that?' enquired the eager skier.

'That is Hell,' replied the saint.

'Some hell,' protested Michael. 'There are no skiing facilities here, and down there is lovely snow, good slopes, a slalom run and a giant slalom, and just look at that mogul field. Wonderful skiing conditions.'

'Ah, but there is no skiing equipment,' chuckled St Peter. 'That's the hell of it!'

The four lady skiers were standing together on a slope when a warning yell made them jump clear as a naked male skier, wearing only a ski mask, sped past them.

'Oh,' gasped one, 'a streaker on the slopes. I wonder who it could be.'

'Not my husband,' stated the second woman.

'He's certainly not my husband,' said the third woman.

'He's not even staying at our hotel,' declared the fourth woman.

The reporter returned to the office with one finger bandaged.

'What happend to you?' asked the editor.

'Frostbite,' replied the reporter.

'How the hell did you get frostbite? I only sent you to cover the opening of the indoor skiing exhibition at Wembley,' growled the editor.

'Well,' explained the reporter, 'the exhibition was opened by Sir David Frost, I had an argument with him, shook my finger at him and he bit it!'

'This ski suit, madam, is designer-made,' said the salesperson in a very haughty manner. 'It costs twelve hundred pounds and guarantees a fit.'

'Oh, at that price it will guarantee a fit all right,' said the customer, 'when my husband hears how much it cost!'

The two women were discussing their holiday plans and one remarked, 'I suppose you're going on a skiing holiday as usual.'

'No, we intend going on a cruise,' replied the second woman.

'A cruise?' queried the first woman. 'That really does surprise

me. I thought John was a ski man. He goes skiing about eight times a year, and never misses.'

'Well, I think John is cured of skiing since he joined Skiers Anonymous,' replied John's wife.

'Skiers Anonymous? I never heard of that.'

'It was formed for ski addicts. When you feel you want to go skiing you telephone a certain number and someone will come to see you and drink with you until you're stoned out of your mind.'

'I was never so humiliated in my life,' stormed the wife, banging the door of the car. 'How could you possibly do such a thing? I'll never be able to face my family again.'

'Well, it's what the man in the sporting equipment shop told me when I bought the new ski boots. He said to wear them as much as possible before going skiing and that would help me get used to them and the proper feel of them,' stated the husband.

'Yes, but not at my sister's wedding!' cried the wife.

The two ladies were discussing their respective skiing holidays.

'The resort where I spent my holiday is terribly chic,' boasted one woman. 'What about your resort, was it chic?'

'Chic? You have no idea,' replied her friend. 'It was so chic if you sprained your wrist they gift-wrapped it!'

The girl unpacked her cases and displayed her new, very trendy ski suits. 'I am determined,' she announced to her female companion, 'that I will attract attention on the slopes during this holiday.'

'Well, you're going the wrong way about it,' advised her girlfriend.

'If this doesn't attract attention,' said the girl, holding up a brightly coloured ski suit, 'what will?'

'Try skiing naked,' suggested her friend.

The skier approached the team manager and complained strongly. 'I see you haven't selected me for the giant slalom and I think that's most unfair. Who better than me for carving a turn?'

'Carving a turn!' shouted the manager. 'John you couldn't carve your own turkey on Christmas Day!'

The man walked into a ski shop and was looking at ski equipment.

'Can I help you, sir?' asked an assistant.

'I was looking for something for my wife.'

'Indeed? What are you asking for her?'

A skier who had taken a nasty fall on the jump hobbled into the lounge at a well-known ski resort and tried to sit on a stool at the bar but had to be helped up by the pretty young girl who was serving the drinks.

'What can I get you?' asked the girl.

'Brandy and ginger please and have something yourself,' replied the injured skier.

'Thank you,' said the girl as she poured the man his drink. 'You've had a nasty accident.'

'Yes, indeed,' answered the man. 'Happened a couple of days ago when I was jumping.'

As he spoke the skier tried to lift his glass but was unsuccessful and the pretty young girl, being very helpful, lifted the glass to his mouth.

'Thank you,' said the man. 'Could you light a cigarette for me?'

'Certainly,' replied the girl and located his cigarettes and lighter in his coat pocket. She selected a cigarette, gently slid it between his lips and snapped the lighter into flame.

'Thank you again,' responded the man as he drew strongly on his cigarette.

For about two hours the girl helped the injured man with his drinks and cigarettes and then he asked, 'Where is the gents' toilet?'

The girl went ashen and stammered, 'Oh, I'm sorry it's out of order. You'll have to go to the one upstairs!'

A friend was consoling the widow of a man who had been killed in a skiing accident. 'Time is a great healer,' she proclaimed.

'I feel rather guilty,' admitted the widow, 'because I persuaded him to go on a skiing holiday.'

'Oh, you mustn't feel like that,' admonished her friend. 'You must now consider yourself. I hope he didn't leave you penniless.'

'On the contrary,' corrected the widow. 'He left me over two million pounds.'

'My goodness!' exclaimed the friend. 'To think he could neither read nor write.'

The widow nodded earnestly and added, 'Nor ski.'

'You know,' said the skiing commentator to his new television assistant, 'it took me about twenty years to realize I knew nothing about skiing.'

'Why didn't you give up commentating?' asked the girl.

'Too late. By that time I was an acknowledged authority on the sport,' shrugged the commentator.

'I don't know,' complained the husband, 'I'm a reasonably good skier but anyone watching me today would think I'd never had a pair of skis on before.'

'Well, you looked good to me,' replied his young, loyal wife. 'I can't ski but you're an excellent skier. Remember yesterday how some of the other skiers remarked how good you were?'

'That's just it,' grumbled her husband. 'One day I'm good, the next day I'm bad, then the next day I'm good, then the next day I'm bad. Just can't understand it.'

'If that's the case,' pointed out his wife brightly, 'why don't you just ski every other day?'

The girl completed the slalom run with all the ability and ease of a very experienced skier and the man following her couldn't match her skill. She was removing her gloves when he joined her.

'That was a wonderful performance,' complimented the man as he pushed up his goggles. 'Really, an excellent show.'

'Thank you,' replied the girl. 'Did you see me complete the run?'

'Oh yes, I was right behind you,' answered the man. 'You're Scottish, aren't you?'

'Yes, I am. How did you know?' smiled the girl.

'The way you roll your Rs,' said the man.

Reading a ski manual is like reading a sex manual – it looks great on paper but when it comes to being in the right position at the right moment it doesn't always come good.

He had been a champion skier for years when he suddenly announced his retirement.

'What are your reasons for retiring?' enquired a reporter.

'I'm retiring on the grounds of illness and fatigue,' answered the champion skier.

'Illness and fatigue?' echoed the surprised reporter.

'Yes. My fans are sick and tired of me,' came the sad reply.

The Irish group stood watching one of their members prepare to jump.

Suddenly he was off.

'Has he fallen?' asked a member of the party.

'No, he's all right,' replied the manager.

'But he can't be,' insisted the member, 'he's upside down and his skis are in the air!'

'That's all right,' replied the team manager. 'I told him to use his head.'

A woman was attending selection for jury service.
'Occupation?'
'Housewife,' she answered.
'Your husband's occupation?' was the next question.
'Manufacturer,' was her reply.
'Children?'
'No, skiing equipment.'

The married couple returned to their hotel room having spent the day skiing. The husband was a very enthusiastic skier and enjoyed every minute of the sport, but his wife was less enthusiastic. She was bruised, cold and every bone in her body ached.

'Skiing is stupid,' she cried as she struggled out of her ski suit.

'You're so right,' agreed her husband. 'I'm glad we don't have to go out again until tomorrow morning.'

Camilla stormed out of the sporting equipment shop announcing, 'I'll never go into that shop again and I'm going to tell all my friends to buy their skiing equipment elsewhere!'

'What happened?' asked her friend.

'I asked the assistant if he had a pair of skis which would

match my fox-hunting pink skiing outfit and he fell about laughing.'

A first-time skier was buying new equipment and clothing in a sporting goods store. He had selected his ski suit, underclothes, goggles, boots, after-ski boots, hat and gloves. He spent some time deciding which skis and poles to purchase but eventually all was settled.

'And this little gift is with our compliments,' said the shop manager, handing the skier a small leather-covered box.

'What is it?' asked the skier.

'It's a little box containing small bottles so you can make a martini and thus expedite your rescue should you get lost or require help,' replied the manager.

'What do you mean, expedite my rescue?' the puzzled skier asked. 'How would making a martini help?'

'Well,' said the manager in a knowing fashion, 'as everyone who has ever made a martini knows, as soon as you start to mix one people will suddenly appear from everywhere to tell you how to do it.'

Recent research shows that Jack and Jill actually went up the hill to ski.

It was one of the larger moguls and the eager skier felt he could ski it at speed. He started off quite well, fine absorbing action, gliding smoothly, straightening, good balance, letting the moguls do the work. As his confidence grew, so did his

speed but suddenly he stiffened and all went wrong. Arms, legs, skis and poles went all over the place as he bounced in the air and landed with a sickening thud. A sharp crack, and he knew his leg was broken.

Just then another skier arrived and, coming to a standstill, asked, 'Have an accident?'

'No, thanks,' muttered the injured skier. 'I've just had one.'

The ski instructor tapped the Irishman on the shoulder and remarked, 'When I said you should sharpen your skis, I meant the edges, not to a point at the front!'

The man went to see a psychiatrist about his dreams.

'Every night I dream about skiing and it's driving me mad,' said the man.

'Don't you ever dream about girls?' asked the psychiatrist.

'What?' shouted the man. 'And miss my turn on the slalom?'

The skier was preparing to ski off-piste when the zipper on the front of his jacket broke. Another skier suggested wearing the jacket back to front and using pins at the back so it would keep out the wind and not flap open. So the skier set off with his back-to-front jacket and was enjoying his skiing when, as he was making a short turn, he lost his balance and fell, rolling over in the snow. His yell as he fell brought an Irish skier to his side to render help.

Soon the two men were joined by the ski patrol who asked the Irishman the extent of the skier's injuries.

'Faith and I don't know,' replied the Irishman. 'He didn't seem too bad until I twisted his head back to the right position and since that he hasn't moved!'

The skier was sitting in the bar, drinking his beer and bemoaning his poor performance on the slopes earlier that day. 'I just can't believe it,' he announced loudly.

'Believe what?' asked his drinking companion.

'That I didn't make that run today,' complained the off-form skier.

'Yes,' nodded his friend , 'reminds me of your cricketing days.'

'How did Robert perform in the ski jump today?' asked the anxious wife.

'He was so long in the air the Royal Air Force should award him his wings,' answered the instructor.

Two pretty girls, one blonde, one redhead, on their first skiing holiday approached a ski instructor.

'Good afternoon,' said the pretty blonde. 'My friend here wants to learn to ski.'

'Certainly,' smiled the instructor, 'and what about you? Do you want to learn?'

'No, thanks,' replied the blonde. 'I learned this morning.'

'Now remember,' said the ski instructor to a young learner, 'skiing develops initiative, reaction to conditions,

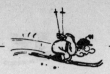

leadership, quick-thinking, self-reliance, spontaneous response, decision-making and quick judgement. So get on to that run and do exactly what I told you!'

'Hello,' said Rodney, lifting the telephone.
'Rodney,' greeted the voice, 'it's Reggie. I've got it made. My wife is away for the week – let's go skiing.'
'Sorry, old chap, I've got it made too,' replied Rodney. 'My wife is away skiing for the week and I have to look after the au pair girl.'

The newcomer to the resort was very much at ease on his skis. He observed all the rules and moved with considerable grace.
'I've seen you here before,' remarked one of the instructors. 'How long have you been skiing?'
'Oh, a couple of months,' was the reply.
'Well, you certainly ski exceptionally well,' praised the instructor.
'I ought to,' declared the skier, 'it took me seven years to learn!'

As a man was lifting a new pair of skis out of his car, his neighbour commented, 'Nice skis.'
'Yes,' replied the man. 'I got them for my wife.'
'Christ!' exclaimed the neighbour. 'That's great. I wish I could make a swop like that!'

A sudden avalanche blocked the homeward run for a number of skiers. The ski patrol, alarmed at so many skiers being missing, requested the local Red Cross Rescue Team to help.

The Red Cross party located a disused cabin and, thinking some of the skiers might have taken refuge there, one of the rescuers hammered on the door and shouted, 'Red Cross here!'

'I've already given,' came the reply from the cabin.

The man slowly shuffled into the office and very gently lowered himself into a chair at his desk.

'Hello, Tim,' greeted a colleague. 'I can see your holiday did you a lot of good. What happened?'

'Straddle sores,' moaned Tim.

'You mean saddle sores,' corrected his friend.

'No, I don't, I mean straddle sores. I went on a skiing holiday,' groaned Tim, trying to get comfortable.

'How do you get straddle sores on a skiing holiday?' asked the puzzled colleague.

'Well, I was skiing a slalom course and as you know there are poles forming gates through which you have to ski,' explained Tim.

'Right. So what?'

'The poles are supposed to be flexible but when I straddled one it wasn't,' came the tearful reply.

'How did they tell you that you had been dropped from the Winter Olympics Team?' enquired an interested friend.

'Oh, very gently,' replied the disappointed skier. 'The team manager came to me and said he wouldn't be seeing me during the games as they didn't allow visitors in the changing rooms.'

The rabbi watched thoughtfully as the priest touched his skis and ski poles, sprinkled holy water over them and muttered to himself.

'What are you doing?' asked the rabbi.

'I am blessing my skis and ski poles,' answered the priest.

'What is the purpose of that?' queried the rabbi.

'So I will ski better and be accident free,' replied the priest.

And the rabbi went away and made an incision in each of his ski poles.

'When I was at school I had a lovely snowboard,' boasted Ronald.

'When I was at school I was too poor to have a snowboard,' admitted John. 'I used to slide downhill on my sister.'

'Don't look so disappointed,' said Liz, putting her arm around Pam's shoulders. 'After all, that was only your first lesson.'

'Oh, it's not the lesson,' replied Pam.

'What is it?' asked Liz.

'Before I came here I heard the absolute minimum was 18 cm, but I didn't realize they were talking about the depth of the snow,' said Pam.

The ski-suited woman stormed into the hotel at the ski resort and went up to the reception desk. 'How soon can I get out of this place and back to England?' she demanded in anger of the reception clerk.

'I will check, madam,' answered the clerk gently. 'Is there something wrong? Something happen to annoy madam?'

'Of course something happened to annoy madam!' shouted the woman.

'What was that, if I may ask?' probed the clerk with extreme politeness.

'One of your instructors told us during a class to improve our turns it was a good ploy to put down a marker and ski around it, he said your hat would do,' thundered the woman.

'That is quite normal, what is wrong with it?' asked the clerk.

'My husband insisted on using my hat,' spat out the woman.

'So?'

'I was wearing it at the time!'

Scott had just returned from a skiing holiday and went to the local Saturday night dance.

As he danced with a pretty young girl he remarked, 'I'm afraid my dancing is not very good this evening. I'm a little stiff from skiing.'

'I think you're nice,' replied the girl, 'and it doesn't make any difference to me where you come from!'

The skier hadn't jumped at all well and asked the team manager, 'What do you think of my execution?'

'I think it's an excellent idea,' growled the manager.

Norman was an average skier with delusions of grandeur and was pleased when he was invited to take part in a biathlon.

He wasn't a good shot, though, so he thought about it for a moment then said, 'No, I can't do it. It might spoil my reputation.'

'That's what I mean,' purred the other skier. 'It's your big chance.'

'I believe Alice didn't do very well on her skiing holiday,' remarked Ken.

'Do well?' echoed Jane. 'She was so bad a ski patrolman clamped her skis!'

Mrs Lewis and Mrs Lynn were on a skiing holiday and as they stood looking out of the hotel window on the first day Mrs Lynn remarked, 'I'll never forget the day my husband and I reached the top of the mountain. His face dropped about a mile.'

'You mean to say he was disappointed?' asked Mrs Lewis incredulously, as she admired the view.

'Oh, no,' Mrs Lynn assured her. 'He fell off the top of the mountain!'

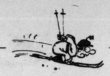

'You are charged with stealing £2,000 worth of skiing equipment,' frowned the magistrate. 'How do you plead?'

'Not guilty by reason of insanity,' answered the man.

'Insanity?' questioned the magistrate.

'Yes. I'm mad about skiing,' came the reply.

Skiers should always be aware of, and abide by, warning signs on the slopes. However, not enough attention is paid to a sign at the entrance to a bar in the ski resort of Aspen, Colorado, which warns:

CAUTION! SOFT SHOULDERS AND DANGEROUS CURVES AHEAD!

Mick and Paddy were about to share a T-bar and Mick noticed Paddy was only wearing one glove.

'Where is your other glove?' asked Mick.

'In the bedroom,' replied Paddy.

'I'll wait for you until you get it,' volunteered Mick, shouldering his skis.

'Oh, I don't need it,' answered Paddy.

'Of course you need it,' pointed out Mick.

'Not according to the weather forecast,' stated Paddy. 'The met man said today would probably be mild but on the other hand it may be cold!'

The two girls were on their first skiing holiday and on the third day Maggie asked if she could wear a skirt when skiing instead of the tight-fitting trousers.

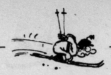

'I don't think a skirt would be suitable,' replied Rita. 'Why don't you want to wear trousers?'

'Well, since I arrived here,' confided Maggie, 'I have been suffering from flatulence and every time I break wind the bindings on my boots come open and my skis fly off!'

M r and Mrs Smith arrived in Switzerland for their first skiing holiday and were greeted by an instructor. 'My name is Rudolph and I will be your instructor.'

'Are you Swiss?' enquired Mrs Smith.

'No, Russian,' was the reply.

'And you came here to teach skiing, how nice,' commented Mrs Smith.

'Well,' said Rudolph, 'I am a member of the Communist Party and when the regime changed I moved here. I love skiing so it suits me.'

'Will we start our lessons today?' asked Mrs Smith.

'Not today,' advised Rudolph, holding out his hands. 'Look, the rain is falling.'

'Looks more like sleet to me,' observed Mrs Smith.

'Now, Nora, don't argue,' cut in Mr Smith. 'Rudolph the Red, knows rain, dear.'

I had to stop watching skiing on television for health reasons,' said Martin.

'Giving you headaches?' sympathized Bob.

'No. My wife threatened to kill me.'

The chair lift jerked to an emergency stop and a ski patrolman ran to a two-seater and yelled at the sole passenger. 'Mr Rourke, your wife fell off three hundred metres back!'

'What?' shouted Mr Rourke.

'Your wife fell off,' repeated the patrolman.

'Oh, thank God for that!' cried Mr Rourke. 'I thought I'd gone deaf!'

'My husband has taken out special insurance to cover him in the event he has a skiing accident. I think they call it double indemnity,' announced Anne.

'Double indemnity?' queried Victoria. 'What does that mean?'

'I think if he is killed in a skiing accident they bury him twice,' said Anne.

'My husband has given up skiing since he was diagnosed as suffering from anuspointphobia,' said Alice.

'My goodness! Whatever is that?' asked Jane.

'The fear of backing into a ski pole,' answered Alice.

'I'm so sorry to hear about the death of your husband,' commiserated Mrs Reid. 'A skiing accident I believe.'

'Yes, he thought he could race an avalanche and beat it,' replied Mrs Dickens. 'He was so wrong. His love of skiing always caused me trouble and still does.'

'Still does?' asked Mrs Reid. 'What do you mean?'

'He wants to be buried wearing his skis,' said Mrs Dickens sadly, shaking her head.

Ron confronted Mike in the bar and poked him in the chest with his finger. 'You really let me down this morning. I had told my friends you were an Irish Ski Champion and when you were on the slopes this morning you acted like a beginner.'

'Shure and I am a ski champion. I'm the Irish Uphill Jump Champion but all the jumps here go down,' replied Mike.

A wife decided to take up skiing so she could accompany her husband on his trips to a ski resort. Her husband took her along to buy skiing equipment and when a shop assistant indicated the skis on the stand the woman raised her hands in protest.

'No! No! No!' the wife exclaimed. 'I want short skis.'

'But those skis are a suitable length,' pointed out her husband.

'Not for me they're not,' declared the wife. 'I'll have to squeeze my foot into shorter skis, I've no intention of letting people know I wear a size seven shoe.'

Penny was sipping her coffee when Sarah joined her for breakfast.

'Good morning, Penny. You were taking skiing lessons late last night,' greeted Sarah as she sat down.

'No, I wasn't,' replied Penny.

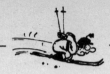

'Well, when I was passing your hotel room about midnight I heard one of the instructors telling you to "Bend ze neeze! Bend ze neeze!" ' said Sarah.

'You probably did,' smiled Penny, 'but I can assure you it had nothing to do with skiing.'

The two girls were in a two-seater chair lift and one confessed, 'I shouldn't be telling you this, but I simply must tell someone. I'm having an affair!'

'Really,' murmured the other girl in a disinterested tone. 'Who is doing the catering?'

'Have you any holiday arrangements made for this year, Mrs Dawson?' enquired Mrs Biggins.

'Oh, yes,' replied Mrs Dawson. 'We have our holidays booked. As you know, we like to ski, so we are going on a skiing holiday.'

'Are you going soon?' asked Mrs Biggins.

'Oh, yes, we like to go at the start of the season before the snow gets dirty,' stated Mrs Dawson.

The man walked into the travel agent and asked if he could book a holiday.

'Certainly, sir,' said the helpful clerk. 'Had you any particular type of holiday in mind? Cruise? America? Far East?'

'No, nothing like that,' answered the man. 'I want a restful holiday.'

'Oh, well then, here are some lovely beach holidays,' said the clerk, opening a holiday brochure.

'No, thank you,' countered the customer. 'I want to book a skiing holiday.'

'A skiing holiday?' echoed the surprised clerk. 'But I thought you said you wanted a restful holiday?'

'I do,' agreed the customer. 'I had a skiing holiday last year and it was very restful. The first day on the slopes and the rest of the holiday in a hospital bed. Wonderful!'

'I'm thinking of taking up skiing,' said Vera. 'You ski a lot, Paul, so perhaps you could advise me on what I need.'

'Certainly,' replied Paul cheerfully. 'To go skiing just make sure you have plenty of white snow and Red Cross.'

The perky young blonde arrived at the ski resort for her second visit and after the first day on the slopes she said to her instructor, 'Well, have you noticed a change since last year?'

'Indeed I have noticed,' confirmed the instructor. 'You've changed your hairstyle!'

The British skier's jump was a terrible effort and the team captain was furious.

'Well, then,' challenged the skier, 'how would you have made the jump?'

'Under an assumed name,' growled the captain through clenched teeth.

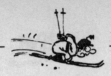

'I thought you were going on a skiing holiday,' said Tom. 'Well,' replied Harry, 'I had thought about taking up skiing but then I decided to let it slide.'

An Irish ski club was holding a special meeting to celebrate the winning of a number of cups for various skiing events: slalom, jump, downhill and biathlon. The president of the club had just finished his congratulatory address when the fire alarm sounded and cries of 'Fire! Fire!' were heard.

'Save the cups!' yelled the president. 'Save the cups!'

So all the members ran to the kitchen.

'My husband received an international award for skiing,' said Doris proudly.

'How wonderful,' excalaimed Grace. 'What was the award?'

'The Noball Prize,' answered Doris.

'You mean the Nobel Prize,' corrected Grace, 'and I didn't think they awarded that prize for skiing.'

'No, it was the Noball Prize,' confirmed Doris. 'He straddled every gate on the giant slalom!'

Mr and Mrs Colman were very worried about their 16-year-old son. For three years he hadn't spoken. Doctors and specialists all agreed they could not give a reason for his lack of speech.

The boy would sit for hours watching skiing on television so Mrs Colman thought it would be a good idea if they took him on a skiing holiday.

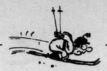

On the first day of the holiday father and son went to the slopes and were preparing for a downhill run when a beautiful blonde in a bright red tight-fitting ski suit bent down to adjust her ski.

'Christ!' exclaimed the son. 'Just look at that arse!'

'You can talk . . . my boy, you can talk!' shouted the excited father.

'Of course I can talk,' replied his son.

'But why didn't you talk before?' questioned his father.

'There was nothing worth talking about,' shrugged the son.

The ski instructor watched the little lady with great interest then asked, 'How long have you been skiing?'

'Well,' said the little lady thoughtfully, 'in six days' time it'll be a week.'

The Irish Ski Trials were in progress and a group of Irish officials was watching the performance of the skiers, making notes and taking times. One skier made a terrible jump, completely lost control and crashed into the group, knocking some of the officials to the ground.

'Help!' cried an Irish timekeeper. 'I've lost an ear! My ear has been cut off!'

'I've found it!' shouted another official, holding up an ear.

'That's not mine,' yelled the timekeeper. 'Mine had a pen behind it!'

'Your husband has a lovely forward position when he's jumping,' remarked a woman to her female companion.

'Oh, he is well used to that position,' replied the wife. 'That's the way he comes home from the pub every night.'

A skier was visiting a politician and noticed an oar displayed on the wall of the study. The politician was quick to notice the observation and explained, 'That's the oar I used in the varsity boat race. We won by a canvas.'

Some time later the politician called to see the skier and saw a pair of skis mounted in the hall. Indicating the skis he asked, 'Which event?'

'The biathlon,' answered the skier.

'Oh, you won the biathlon,' exclaimed the politician. 'Jolly good!'

'No, I didn't win the biathlon,' replied the skier. 'Those are the skis worn by the winner. I accidentally shot him!'

As Penny was passing the market stall she saw some very inexpensive ski pants. Always ready for a bargain, she examined the pants and was assured by the Indian stallholder that they were excellent value.

'Right, I'll take a pair,' said Penny, handing over the money.

'You will not be sorry,' advised the salesman. 'They will also be very lucky for you.'

The following day Penny went on her skiing holiday and wore her new ski pants but to her horror and mortification the seams of the pants split, providing the best scenery of the day.

On her return home she took the pants back to the stallholder and, waving the defective article at him, cried, 'I was done in these ski pants!'

'Ah,' said the Indian stallholder, pressing his hands together and nodding his head. 'I told you they would be lucky for you.'

Working on the principle that you meet the 'right' kind of people on the ski slopes, Mrs Cohen sent her 8-year-old son, Isaac, to a ski school for four weeks. She was distressed when three days later the chief instructor telephoned her and requested she come and take her son home as he was not interested in skiing.

'But that is nonsense,' shouted Mrs Cohen, 'he must be interested in skiing. He knows it will benefit him.'

'He has no interest in learning to ski,' said the chief instructor firmly. 'He doesn't want to attend classes and if he does attend, he has a disruptive influence on the other pupils. All he is doing is wasting your money and our time and we do have to think of the school's reputation.'

'Do you think I should speak to him?' enquired a concerned Mrs Cohen.

'I don't think that would make any difference,' answered the instructor. 'He doesn't want to ski. This morning he didn't attend class and we had to search for him. We eventually found him in one of the storerooms playing with his genitals.'

'Well,' exclaimed Mrs Cohen in triumph, 'that can't be a bad thing. Some of my best friends are genitals!'

The skier had been involved in a horrendous car crash which resulted in the amputation of his right leg.

One day in hospital as he was standing by his bed leaning on a cane, he was approached by a male visitor who introduced himself as Roddy Lloyd.

'I know you by reputation, Mr Lloyd,' said the injured skier. 'You've won about every skiing trophy there is.'

'Well, I've won quite a few,' replied the modest Mr Lloyd, 'and that's why I'm here to see you. I know you are a keen skier and are probably depressed at present owing to your injuries and I just wanted to tell you I won all my skiing competitions after I had been fitted with an artificial leg.'

'I didn't know that,' said the skier.

'Not many people do,' smiled Mr Lloyd. 'So you see, the loss of a leg shouldn't stop you skiing. Matter of fact, it has the advantage that you don't feel any pain in that leg.'

'I never thought of that,' declared the young skier.

'Here, I'll show you,' offered Roddy Lloyd. 'Hit me as hard as you can on the leg with your cane.'

The young skier steadied himself, swung the cane and struck Lloyd's leg.

'Christ Almighty!' yelled Lloyd in pain as he fell to the floor. 'You hit the wrong bloody leg!'

'I'd like stilts for Christmas,' said the little boy.

'But, darling,' pointed out his mother, 'Santa Claus would never get them down the chimney.'

'I don't see why not,' replied her son. 'He got Daddy's skis down last year.'

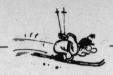

'I say, George takes those left-hand turns very well,'
remarked one observer to his companion as they watched
a skier on the slalom. 'Must put in a hell of a lot of training.'

'Not really,' answered his companion. 'That's the way he
leans on the bar.'

'Hello, Tom,' greeted Dick. 'Is it true you were told you
couldn't take part in the British Ski Championship
because you used steroids?'

'Not true, Dick,' replied Tom. 'I was told I couldn't take
part in the Ski Championship because I had haemorrhoids!'

The woman was on a charge of murdering her husband
by stabbing him with a ski and was being questioned by
a barrister.

'Why did you kill your husband?' came the question from
the barrister.

'I meant nothing to him. All he could think of was skiing,'
sobbed the woman. 'We had a terrible row and I told him
he would have to choose one or the other, his skiing or me.
He said he would take the skiing so I grabbed a ski and stabbed
him.'

'This is completely beyond my comprehension,' stated the
barrister.

'What appears to be your problem in understanding the
situation?' rumbled the judge.

'M'lud, why this woman should stab her husband with a
ski when a ski pole would have been much more suitable is
quite beyond me,' voiced the barrister.

'What's this I hear about Maud suing the council under the Trades Description Act about their skiing facilities?' asked Susan.

'Well, she went to one of their dry slopes and it rained,' replied Sally.

The married couple had gone off-piste and crashed down a ravine. They tried to climb out but the wife couldn't manage to do so. The husband was more successful and had just pulled himself clear as the rescue team arrived.

'Are you all right?' enquired the team leader.

'Yes, fine,' replied the husband.

'Why didn't you help your wife to get out?' asked the team leader.

'I couldn't,' replied the husband. 'I had to carry my skis!'

Paddy and Bridget were enjoying the freedom of off-piste skiing when Paddy failed to see a warning sign and fell down a ravine. Bridget went for help and the rescue team soon arrived and hoisted Paddy from the depths of the ravine to ground level and laid his still form on a stretcher.

As a doctor examined the injured skier Bridget anxiously asked, 'How is he, doctor?'

'Oh, madam, I regret to say this but I think he is dead,' replied the doctor gravely.

Just then Paddy slowly opened one eye and croaked softly, 'Bridget, I'm not dead.'

'Now, Paddy,' said Bridget sternly, 'if the doctor says you're dead – you're dead!'

Pam arrived at the smart ski resort in Switzerland and rushed to meet her friend Clare, who had just completed the slalom.

'I've just got here and this is my first time,' smiled Pam, 'so tell me about the gates.'

'Certainly,' said Clare. 'Any particular gates . . . Camillagate, Charlesgate, Dianagate, Squidgygate or Fergiegate?'

Famous Last Words For Skiers

- 'I just looked back.'

- 'Frankly, the crevasse didn't seem so very wide.'

- 'I couldn't find the fall-line.'

- 'I thought a schuss was a little German dog.'

- 'I'll wave to you as I jump.'

- 'I never pay attention to warning signs.'

- 'No, dear, you won't be able to carry your duty free items in the basket on your ski pole.'

- 'How was I to know hot-dogging had nothing to do with mustard?'